# Racism

# What's That Got To Do With Me?

# Racism

Antony Lishak

FRANKLIN WATTS
LONDON•SYDNEY

First published in 2005 by
Franklin Watts
96 Leonard Street
London
EC2A 4XD

Franklin Watts Australia
Level 17/207 Kent Street
Sydney NSW 2000

Series editor: Adrian Cole
Design: Thomas Keenes
Art director: Jonathan Hair
Picture researcher: Diana Morris

A CIP catalogue record for this book is
available from the British Library.

ISBN: 0 7496 6396 0

Dewey Classification: 305.8

Printed in China

Acknowledgements:
Bettmann/Corbis: 25l. Bristol Evening Post: 16. Esbin-
Anderson/Image Works/Topham: 14. Everett Collection/Rex
Features: 11. Chris Gray/Image Works/Topham. Posed by
models: 6c & 22. Sally & Richard Greenhill/Alamy: front cover
b, back cover b, 6cr, 26. Harper's Weekly 1876: 27. B.
Heger/Exile Images: front cover t, back cover t, 4-5, 17.
Ralf Finn Hestoft/Corbis: 15. Owen Humpreys/PA. Empics: 1, 2,
7, 31, 32. Andrew Jankunas/Alamy: 8, 28l. Andrew
McCafferty/Rex Features: 12, 28c. Popperfoto/Alamy: 21. Rex
Features: 19. Roger-Viollet/Topham: 13. Ron Ryan/Cooee
Picture Archive: 9. Sipa Press/Rex Features: 24, 29. Topham:
23. Penny Tweedie/Alamy. Posed by model: 20.Peter M
Wilson/Alamy: 18. David Young-Wolff/Alamy: 6cl, 10, 28cl.

Whilst every attempt has been made to clear copyright.
Should there be any inadvertent omission please apply in the
first instance to the publisher regarding rectification.

# Contents

# So what?

As soon as we meet someone new we categorise them – it's natural. Within seconds we have noted if they are male or female, and also their age, skin colour, height, clothes, hair and so on. It's when we start to make judgements about that person, based on these categories, that problems occur.

## What's it all about?

Racism is when a person is judged and then discriminated against because of their skin colour, nationality, culture or religion. Unfortunately, many of us will experience racism in one form or another during our lives. On the following pages you will hear from a selection of people whose lives have been shaped in different ways by racial prejudice: a football fan, a self-confessed racist, someone who was snatched at birth, and a young girl who was caught in a racial dilemma.

## Personal accounts

All of the testimonies are true. Some are first-hand accounts, while others are the result of bringing similar experiences together to create a single "voice". Every effort has been made to ensure they are authentic. To protect identities, a few names have been changed and models have posed for some of the pictures. Wherever possible, permission to use the information has been obtained.

## Ask yourself

The testimonies won't tell you all there is to know about racism, that wouldn't be possible. Instead, as you encounter the views of the people featured in this book, think about your own opinions and experiences. This will help you begin to address the question: "Racism – what's that got to do with me?"

Tension over racial discrimination in Bradford, UK, led to this riot in 2001.

# An immigrant

When people migrate to a different country, aspects of their home life are different from those of other people in society. It is sometimes hard for children to balance their lives between these two influences.

My name is Sara Wai Hsien Man, my mum and dad are Chinese but I was born in Australia. Growing up in two communities was difficult at first. My appearance stopped me feeling 100% Australian, and I wasn't completely at home in Chinese surroundings either.

My first big shock was when I went to school – I was the only oriental child there. Not being able to speak a single word of English was very frustrating. Sometimes other children would say hurtful things, but I learnt to cope; I once even pretended I knew some kung fu moves to scare off bullies.

At home my parents preferred to speak Chinese, while I expressed myself best in English. I couldn't understand why

This Australian woman balances her life between Australian and Chinese influences.

## Fact bank

■ There are over 30 million people of Chinese origin living outside China. The first Chinese immigrants arrived in Australia in the 1850s. Today there are two "China towns" in Australia, in Melbourne and Sydney, where many of the these people settled. Mandarin Chinese is the language spoken at home for over 300,000 people in Australia.

People in Melbourne, Australia, celebrate Chinese New Year.

they made me go to Chinese school at weekends when my friends were outside enjoying themselves. They spent almost every waking hour working and made sure that I always studied hard at school. It puzzled me then, but now I realise that they wanted me to have a better life.

Now I can see how all the new challenges I had to face as a child made me stronger. I have come to celebrate the variety of experiences that have made me the person I am, and I think I have the best of both worlds.

## Ask yourself this...

■ Why do you think Sara's parents didn't help her to "fit in" to the Australian way of life?

■ How could the staff at Sara's school have helped her to settle in?

■ Over the generations, how many different cultures have merged to make you and your family the people you are today?

■ Do you think Sara would identify herself as Chinese-Australian or Australian-Chinese? How would you describe your own cultural identity?

# A best friend

Adults are meant to know best. But what happens when you know an adult is wrong? Here's a situation that shows how some peoples' opinions have changed over the generations. What would you do?

My name is Joanne, I am 9 years old. Tizzie is my best friend. We play together a lot, especially after school. Her house is right next to the park, so we play on the swings and then go to her house for dinner. She has a new baby brother called Nathan.

Yesterday was my birthday party. My nan came all the way from Scotland to be there. But I wasn't allowed to invite Tizzie. I was very sad because I knew it wouldn't be the same without her. We always go to each other's parties – it's so important. At first Mum said that there wouldn't be enough room (all my cousins were coming to see our nan).

Joanne and Tizzie are the best of friends.

# Fact bank

■ In the past, some people thought is was acceptable for black people to be treated differently from white people. For example, in many places black people were only allowed access to poorly paid work. In the 1960s the campaign to secure civil rights for all citizens of the USA was led by Martin Luther King Junior.

**Martin Luther King Jr at a civil rights meeting, USA.**

But one extra person wouldn't make a difference! I stayed in my room and cried. My mum came upstairs and said that we could have our own special party after school – just the two of us. But I wanted to see Tizzie on my birthday! Then Mum told me the truth. "It would upset your nan – she's a bit funny about black people." I didn't know what to say, it didn't make any sense. "Some old people are like that," she said.

I got lots of presents but I didn't really enjoy myself. It was good to have all the family together, but I missed Tizzie. At school, I told her about what my mum said. She was surprised, but she said that she knew I don't think like that, so we are still best friends.

## Ask yourself this...

■ If you were Joanne, what would you have said to your mum, your nan or to Tizzie? Does respecting your parents always mean you have to accept what they say?

■ Why did Joanne tell Tizzie about the things her mum said?

# A football fan

**Being part of a crowd doesn't stop you from being responsible for your individual actions. At football matches, verbally abusing black players is still a very public form of racism – but anti-racism campaigns are beginning to change some attitudes.**

I was at a football match in 1987 when there were men outside with sacks of bananas. They were handing them out to passing spectators. "It's for the monkey," they were saying. They meant John Barnes of Liverpool – in those days it was quite rare for teams to have black players. I saw quite a few people take them. The idea was to throw the fruit onto the pitch and make ape-like noises when he got the ball. It was so humiliating. I was standing next to one man who shouted: "Go back to the jungle Barnesy!" Lots of people laughed. I didn't, but I was too frightened to tell him to stop.

I thought things were different now. Most teams have players from all over the world and every club supports the "Kick Racism out of Football" campaign – but recently I heard John Barnes on the radio:

"I don't think the situation has gone away or improved. It's just got quieter. If you tell a racist that for 90 minutes on a Saturday that they have to keep their mouth shut, and the other six days and 22-and-a-half hours they can be a racist, I don't see how that's doing anything to stop it."

John Barnes feels that things haven't really changed.

# Fact bank

■ In the USA in 1946, Jackie Robinson became the first black man to play in the previously all-white Major League Baseball (MLB), and was racially abused by some people in the crowd. Whereas today, about 80% of professional basketball players and 66% of American Football players are black, only 10% of the MLB are black.

■ In the UK, although there are now over 300 black professional football players, there are only a few Asian professionals.

**Jackie Robinson faced racial abuse from the crowd.**

# Ask yourself this...

**"Stand up, speak up" wrist bands. These are part of a recent anti-racism campaign.**

■ Just as it takes courage to stand up to a bully, it's difficult to speak out when you see someone else being racist. But if you say nothing how would your silence be interpreted by the racist and their victim?

And what if the racist is one of your friends?

■ How effective do you think anti-racist campaigns like "Stand-up, speak out" really are?

# A concerned mother

Most people agree that there should be no racial discrimination in the police force. We should all be treated the same. But as this mother discovered, it doesn't always happen.

If a police officer thought that someone was about to commit a crime, they would stop and question them – they might even search them – I have no problem with that. But in my experience it isn't always what the person is doing that makes the police think that they are up to no good – it's what they look like. I have four sons, my youngest is adopted. They are all grown up now. When they were teenagers the three older boys were never stopped by the police, but it happened to Darren regularly. He was one of the few black people who lived in our town.

## Fact bank

■ In the USA the police use "racial profiling" to target specific groups of the community when stopping people. About 32 million black and Hispanic Americans report they have been a victim of such profiling. A British government document, released in July 2004, stated that in Britain: "Black people are six times more likely to be searched by police than white people. There are almost twice as many searches of Asian people than white people."

Many people, like this woman, feel that police officers target people from ethnic minorities unfairly.

A US police officer assigned to a special gang unit stops a group of youths.

Darren was the only kid who was told by the police to stop riding his skateboard on the pavement. None of his white friends seemed to attract the same attention. Once late at night, when he was putting his bike in the garage, he was approached by two police officers who assumed he was stealing it. When he told them that this was his house, they didn't believe him and started to shout. I was woken by the noise and came outside. We made a complaint to the police and they apologised. But the whole episode made Darren even more distrustful of the police.

## Ask yourself this...

■ What difference would it have made if the police officers who assumed Darren was stealing the bike were black?

■ What can be done to prevent the police from making similar mistakes?

■ Do you know anyone like Darren that has been the victim of racial discrimination? What happened?

# An asylum seeker

Thousands of people escape persecution by fleeing to another country – it's called "seeking asylum". But to stay and be granted asylum, it must be proved that they were in danger, which can take several years. During this time, life for asylum seekers can be very difficult.

Miguel is eight years old. His mother escaped from Colombia in Central America in fear of her life. When Miguel was four she sought asylum in the UK and while she was waiting for her case to be heard, she found a place for him at a local school.

Early one morning, without warning, the police arrived at the house where they were staying. They took them to a detention centre from which, they were told, they would be sent back to Columbia. It had a traumatic effect on Miguel.

Here is the letter that his school received a few days later:

**mum and son facing return to Colombia**

**Miguel and his mother were happy living in the UK.**

Sorry I didn't come to shool because I am in the detention centre in Gatwick. Well someone ringed on my door at 6 a clock in the morning. It was the Home office with 7 police ofercers and they followed me when I brushed my teeth. I got arrested but without hand cuffs but I didn't do anything wrong.

So they took me to Somerset in a normal car then they dropped me off at a police station. And then we waited till a van came. It was a criminal van. It had double door so no criminals could escape. The van was big...

I am tired now so I will write to you tomorrow. Best wishes Miguel

# Fact bank

■ In 2002, 140 countries signed an agreement promising to provide a place of safety – or asylum – for people who are being persecuted on the basis of race, religion or nationality. Despite this, asylum seekers are often seen as a threat and a burden to the society they try to settle in. In total, there are about 15 million displaced people in the world – Asia provides asylum for 45% of them, Africa 30%, Europe 19% and North America 5%.

**Asylum seekers are interviewed when they first arrive in a new country.**

# Ask yourself this...

■ Is "home" where you were born, where you live, or where your parents come from?

■ How do you think Miguel felt in this situation? Why do you think his letter feels as though it's unfinished?

■ Why do you think some people might feel threatened by asylum seekers?

# A Romany Gypsy

For centuries Romany Gypsies have maintained their travelling lifestyle in many countries, especially in Europe. This way of life has resulted in them being seen as outsiders by many other people. As we hear in this testimony, they still face racial discrimination.

**Roma people live a nomadic lifestyle.**

"Know them before judging them," that's what the new slogan says. It's on the television, on T-shirts and on baseball caps. I really hope it helps to change things because I am one of "them", a Romany Gypsy, or "gitano" as we are known here in Spain.

I live near Barcelona but when I visit the city centre I am not welcome. Sometimes when I go into a shop, they see my dark skin and refuse to serve me. On buses, even though I have a

## Fact bank

■ The origins of the 12 million or so Roma people in the world can be traced back to India over 1,000 years ago. The Romany language has its origins in ancient Punjabi. As Roma people have travelled over the centuries, they have adapted to the different cultures they have encountered, but they still lead a distinctive way of life. There are many groups of people who choose to live "nomadic", or traveller, lifestyles; the Roma people are one of these groups.

ticket, sometimes the driver will tell me to get off. The other passengers just stare in silence, but I know inside they are just like the driver. Only once has another person stood up for me, but then nearly everyone told her to be quiet and mind her own business.

To me there is a double standard here. Everywhere in Barcelona there are the sights and sounds of Flamenco; the music, the art and the dance [of the Roma people]. It is celebrated as a big part of Spanish culture. I see it as a gift from my people to the whole of Spain, but it feels as if it has been stolen from us.

## Ask yourself this...

■ Why do you think only one person on the bus spoke out? And why do you think others told her to mind her own business?

■ Why do you think some people are nomadic? Should they be encouraged to settle in one place? Why might this cause problems?

■ Why do you think this person feels their culture has been stolen?

**Traditionally, Roma people lived in horse-drawn caravans. Now though, many travel in large, modern mobile homes like these.**

# A stolen child

**In Australia, up until the 1970s, some Aboriginal children were taken from their families and brought up as "white". This is the story of one of the "stolen children".**

They took me away to the orphanage when I was a baby. They said my mum was not fit to look after me and didn't even want to know me. It was the same with all of us – they just told us not to even think about our families. They kept telling us we were white. They drummed it into our heads. But we weren't treated like real white kids. My teacher said: "No matter what you learn in class, you'll only ever be good for serving and scrubbing."

Then one day a whole group of black women came to the home. They were looking for their children, but they were turned away. So they sneaked around

**This woman was a young child when she was taken to live in a settlement.**

## Fact bank

■ Between 1900 and 1970, thousands of Aboriginal children were "stolen" from their families and sent to live in state-run "native settlements", where they were taught to ignore their own language and culture. Children were chosen on the basis of skin colour, in the belief that lighter "mixed into the hills and we all went to them. They said they were our mothers, I thought "I ain't got a black mother – I'm white". I had become blind to my own colour. Then my mother called my name, and I went to her. They had told me she was a terrible monster, but she was beautiful. We hugged and this hot rush from the tip of my toes up to my head filled every part of my body. I was 14 and it was the first time I had ever felt love.

That was the last day I saw her alive. When she died, two years later, I was allowed to go to her funeral. I will never forgive them – I was only allowed to see her when she was dead.

## Ask yourself this...

■ According to the Universal Declaration of Human Rights (a document endorsed by most of the nations of the world) "All human beings are born free and equal in dignity and rights". What do you think this Aboriginal woman would have to say about that?

■ Do you think that you have equal rights? How can you tell?

■ Why do you think that Aboriginal people want the present Australian government to apologise for what was done in the past?

race" children could be absorbed into white society. Although this practice is now seen as totally unacceptable, the present Australian government refuses to apologise for the actions of its predecessors.

**Aboriginal people at a native settlement.**

# A racist attitude

There are some people who think that each racial group should live in separate areas, and that the more different cultures mix the weaker they become. Here is the voice of one such person.

I suppose you can call me a racist, but I am also a peaceful white man who just wants to get on with his life. I don't ask black or Asian people to change their culture, I just don't want anything to do with them. In my ideal world, everyone would live in a neighbourhood, and go to work with, their own sort of people. I want my grandson to marry a white girl and have white kids that go to a white school. And when they are there I want them to learn about their own culture.

Look, I don't wish anyone any harm, but I reckon if things carrying on the way they are, and different races continue mixing together, it's all going to boil over.

Isn't the world big enough for us all to live in our own countries? I know a lot of people who would gladly buy plane tickets that would send non-white families back to their own lands.

**This man would prefer to stay separate from other races.**

**Separate toilets for black and white people in South Africa in the 1980s.**

# Fact bank

■ The man in the story (left) suggests keeping different races separate. A policy of racial segregation, called Apartheid, was adopted by the South African government from 1948–92. White people, despite being in the minority, controlled the government, laws and many businesses.

■ Today in South Africa, white and black people have equal rights.

# Ask yourself this...

■ Members of the same ethnic minority group often live in the same area. What affects do you think this has on racial integration?

■ How would your life be affected if this man's "ideal world" became a reality?

■ Why do you think most people find his attitude unacceptable?

# A holocaust survivor

History is filled with examples of extreme racist persecution. Attempts have been made to uproot entire ethnic groups, and in some cases wipe them out. Here, a survivor of the Holocaust (the Nazi's attempt to murder other ethnic groups) remembers her experiences as a child.

I can tell you what happened to me, but I can't tell you why. Of course, it was because I'm a Jew and to be Jewish in Czechoslovakia [now called the Czech Republic] in 1939 was very dangerous. But that doesn't explain how people could be so cruel to one another.

When the Nazis came we were herded into train trucks like cattle and taken away. Just think, one truck crammed with 50 people; no food or drink and one bucket in the middle as a toilet. It was hell – but it was only the beginning.

This woman holds a picture of her taken in a death camp.

## Fact bank

■ Adolf Hitler's Nazi Party came to power in the early 1930s, when there were over 9 million Jews in Europe. In the early 1940s, the Nazis put their "final solution" into action, a policy of "cleansing" Europe of Jews,

We arrived in a place called Auschwitz – a death camp. We were pushed and kicked and shouted at. Then the selection began. Those who were to live (for now) to one side and those who were to die to the other. That meant the gas chambers – it was the last time I saw my father.

I watched my family die. I saw so many terrible things done by one human being to another that I stopped feeling. Imagine, watching someone being shot through the head and feeling nothing.

## Ask yourself this...

■ The world only learnt of the full horrors of the Holocaust after it happened. How do you think racially motivated acts, such as breaking windows in a Jewish-owned shop, can lead to events such as the Holocaust?

■ What do you think this Holocaust survivor would think of the racial hatred that still exists in the world over 60 years after the end of the Second World War?

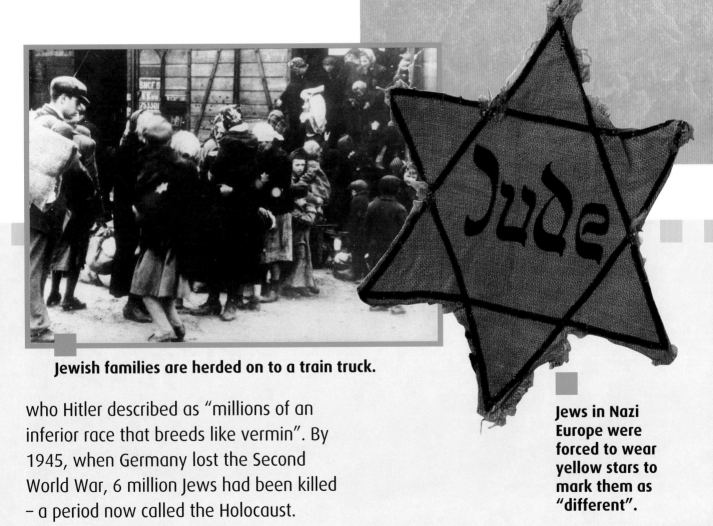

**Jewish families are herded on to a train truck.**

**Jews in Nazi Europe were forced to wear yellow stars to mark them as "different".**

who Hitler described as "millions of an inferior race that breeds like vermin". By 1945, when Germany lost the Second World War, 6 million Jews had been killed – a period now called the Holocaust.

# A playground joker

"Sticks and stones may break my bones but words can never hurt me" – is that true? And what about jokes – can they be hurtful as well? This child has had to think about these questions.

I was with my friends in the playground and they were telling jokes. I told one about a man who goes into a pub and says to the barman – "I just heard the best Irish joke ever," and the barman says, "Before you go on, I'm going to warn you that I'm Irish, and so is nearly everyone in this place." So the

Girls share a joke in a playground. Some jokes can cause people offence.

# Fact bank

■ Many people feel that if a joke is based on a person's race, and told in an offensive way, it is a form of racial harassment. Racial harassment, like racial discrimination, is against the law.

■ To appear funny, some jokes depend on false racially-based assumptions (such as all Irish people are unintelligent). If these assumptions aren't challenged they could easily, but wrongly, be seen as true.

**A US cartoon c.1870. Do false, racially based assumptions still exist today?**

man says, "Okay, then, I'll tell it really slowly."

One of the teachers heard me and told me off for being racist. I said it was only a joke, but he said it wasn't funny. He said that jokes like that only make everyone think that all Irish people are stupid.

After school he gave me a letter to give to my parents asking them to talk to me about using offensive language in school. I don't know what they are going to say. The joke is one of my dad's favourites – and he comes from Ireland!

## Ask yourself this...

■ What do you think her father will say when he reads the letter? Does the fact that her dad is actually Irish make the joke less offensive?

■ Compare this story with the one on pages 24–25. How do you think racially abusive words could lead to the persecution of an entire race?

■ How much does it matter if a joke is offensive, as long as it is funny?

# What does racism have to do with me?

Unfortunately, many people still experience some form of racism – through discrimination, inequality and harassment. Perhaps you've told a joke that people thought was racist, or you know someone that has been a victim of a racially motivated crime. Even if you're lucky enough not to have direct experience of racism, like the people quoted on these two pages, you will still have opinions about it. To find out more look at the websites. They will also help you to answer these questions. Look back through the book, too. Use all this information to form your own opinion about racism.

## In your opinion, is racism a big problem in the world today?

"Racism is man's gravest threat to man – the maximum of hatred for a minimum of reason."
- Abraham Joshua Heschel (Jewish teacher, author and civil rights activist, 1907–72)

"The white man is our mortal enemy, and we cannot accept him."
- Louis Farrakhan (minister and former leader of the Nation of Islam, born 1933)

■ www.myjewishlearning.com
■ www.un.org/WCAR/

**Do you always treat everyone the same – even if they shared the same view as the man on page 18?**

"Yes, I do believe in the inequality of races!"
  – Jean-Marie Le Pen (President of the French National Front, born 1928)

"I have fought against white domination, and I have fought against black domination. I have cherished the ideal of a democratic and free society in which all persons live together in harmony and with equal opportunities. It is an ideal, which I hope to live for and to achieve. But if needs be, it is an ideal for which I am prepared to die."
  – Nelson Mandela (former President of South Africa, born 1918)

■ www.nelsonmandela.org
■ www.annefrank.org/content.asp?
  pid=1&lid=2

**If you heard a friend make a racist comment would you react like the football fan on page 10?**

"If the moderates ... fail to act now, history will have to record that the greatest tragedy ... was not the strident clamour of the bad people, but the appalling silence of the good people."
  – Dr Martin Luther King, Jnr (Nobel peace prize-winning civil rights activist, 1929–68)

"Negroes and whites are different races. We have between us a broader difference than exists between any other two races!"
  – Abraham Lincoln (sixteenth President of the United States, 1809–65)

■ www.kickitout.org
■ www.nike.com/standupspeakup/
  en/home. jsp?page=home

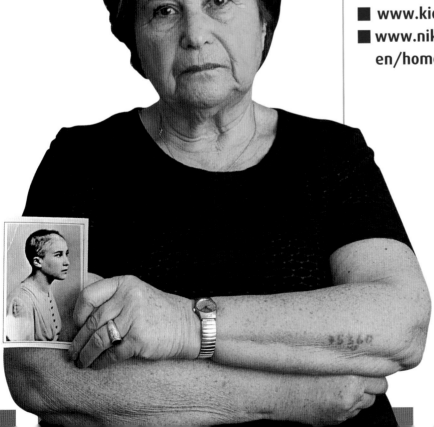

# Websites

The websites below feature more information, news articles and stories that you can use to help form your own opinions. Use the information carefully and consider the source it comes from before drawing any conclusions.

**www.cre.gov.uk**
The website of the Commission for Racial Equality. It includes hot topics and details of current campaigns.

**www.civilrights.org**
This website brings together the work of several different organisations providing up-to-the-minute civil rights news and information.

**www.dreamtime.net.au/ indigenous/social**
Part of the Australian Museum Online website, this "social justice" section features a wide range of information about Australia's Aboriginal population.

**www.civilrightsmuseum.org**
Website of the National Civil Rights Museum in Memphis, USA. Features include online exhibitions and photographs.

**www.voicesofcivil rights.org/**
This website features a wide range of personal accounts and stories from people involved in the struggle for civil rights. It also includes historical information, a timeline and a gallery.

**www.irr.org.uk**
Online news articles from the Independent Race Relations News Network.

# Glossary

**Aboriginal** – original inhabitants of Australia.

**Apartheid** – government policy in South Africa that made racial segregation legal.

**Asylum** – refuge from suffering and persecution.

**Civil rights** – laws that aim to ensure freedom and equality for everyone.

**Culture** – history and traditions that characterise a specific group of people.

**Detention centre** – secure place were asylum seekers are often held.

**Dilemma** – a tricky and often sensitive problem.

**Discrimination** – when a person, or group of people, are treated unfairly.

**Endorsed** – supported.

**Ethnic** – sharing the same cultural and racial identity.

**Flamenco** – vibrant dancing and music from Romany Gypsy culture.

**Gas chambers** – rooms in which holocaust victims were murdered.

**Hispanic** – of Spanish or Latin-American origin.

**Nazi Party** – political group that ruled Germany from 1933–1945.

**Nomadic** – a lifestyle that involves moving from place to place.

**Persecution** – when people are treated unjustly.

**Racial harassment** – when people are abused because of their race.

**Racial prejudice** – act of discriminating against people, on grounds of their race.

**Verbal racial abuse** – when people are insulted or shouted at because of their race.

**www.un.org/av/photo/ subjects/apartheid.htm**
Picture-led part of the United Nations website focusing on the years of Apartheid in South Africa.

**www.romani.org**
Website dedicated to the recognition of the Roma people. It includes information about their history, music and dance.

**www.kickitout.org**
Home of the "Kick Racism Out of Football" campaign, featuring interviews with football players and the latest news updates.

Every effort has been made by the Publishers to ensure that these websites contain no inappropriate or offensive material. However, because of the nature of the Internet, it is impossible to guarantee that the contents of these sites will not be altered. We strongly advise that Internet access is supervised by a responsible adult.

# Index